"... poems of diamond-like brilliance, filled with despair, passion, and surreal beauty. The poet ... in an act of intellectual courage, climbs up on the rubble of western culture to speak truth to both power and powerlessness."
— MARY MACKEY, author of *Sugar Zone* and the novel *The Village of Bones*

"Another entrancing book from a poet and novelist of visionary authority, whose imagination is at once brilliant and unsettling."
— ERNEST HILBERT, author of *Caligulan*

"An attempt to right the world ... a generous collection."
— SIMON PERCHIK

"An extraordinary, and extraordinarily strange, accomplishment. It is bound to offend at least one of your friends."
— JACK FOLEY

" 'The Wife of the Painter' ... takes my breath away. ... 'Midnight' is ... a masterpiece, yet so modest as to almost escape notice."
— CURT BARNES

"In this provocative collection of poems, Christopher Bernard emerges as a maverick bucking current tastes and trends ... balancing an unabashed prophetic fury with poems of great love and tenderness."
— PHILIP FRIED

Chien Lunatique

OTHER BOOKS BY THE AUTHOR

Novels:
A Spy in the Ruins
Voyage to a Phantom City

Short Stories:
In the American Night
Dangerous Stories for Boys

Poetry:
The Rose Shipwreck: Poems and Photographs

Play:
The Beast and Mr. James

Chapbooks:
The Dilettante of Cruelty
Gilded Abattoir
The Blot on the Colophon

Chien Lunatique

Poems

By Christopher Bernard

A *Caveat Lector* Book

REGENT PRESS
Berkeley, California

Copyright © 2017 by Christopher Bernard

[paperback]
ISBN 13: 978-1-58790-380-9
ISBN 10: 1-58790-380-6

[e-book]
ISBN 13: 978-1-58790-381-6
ISBN 10: 1-58790-381-4

Library of Congress Catalog Number: 2016963482

"An Ahumanist," "Modern," "The Invention of Fire" and "The Wife of the Painter" first appeared (in some cases, in slightly different versions) in *Synchronized Chaos*.

"Salt," "A Mistake Somewhere," "Café Kabul" and "Nomad of Love" first appeared (in some cases, in slightly different versions) in *Caveat Lector*.

Cover photograph by the author.

Manufactured in the U.S.A.

REGENT PRESS
Berkeley, California
www.regentpress.net

CONTENTS

Black Fire *9*

The Labyrinth in the Living Room

Vanishing *13*
Self-Identity *16*
The King of the Web *17*
Saint Porn *20*
The Young Man Reviews Books on YouTube *23*
Modern Taste *25*
Paderewski *26*
Victory Cocktail *28*
What Is Literature? *29*

Love Among the Existentialists

The Invention of Fire *35*
Aubade *38*
Botticelli of the Amazon *40*
Nomad of Love *42*
Rite of Spring *47*
Unseason *49*
There's Nothing You Can Give Me *50*
Bocca Baciata *51*
Café Kabul *53*
The Wife of the Painter *55*
Sleeping Beauty *57*
A Beautiful Lie *58*
Fado *60*
A Strindberg of Our Time *61*
Beauty: A Curse *65*

    Love's Labors Lost *68*
    Hotel *69*
    Divorced Children (a fragment) *71*
    Midnight *72*
    Poems *73*
    The Bright Margin *74*

Suicide Machine

    Modern *79*
    A Devil's Bargain *81*
    All You Can Eat at the 21st Century Café *90*
    An Ahumanist *93*
    A Mistake Somewhere *96*
    Blithe Master *100*
    How to Deal with the Brothers Koke *103*
    Salt *106*
    War Poem *108*
    The Hound of Afghanistan *109*
    Eyeless in Gaza *110*
    Six Animal Songs from the Gone World *111*

    Ripped from the Annals *123*

Aujourd'hui il faut être absolument anti-moderne.
— ANTI-RIMBAUD

Black Fire

He belonged to the charming, hopeless breed
of obsessive scribblers whom nobody reads
(present company excepted). He said this to me
without bitterness: "There are too many of us; screeds
we've enough of—just precious few witnesses.

It's my own fault—I admit it: I forgot
to 'kill my darlings.' Portentous words!
I should have aimed at my reader's heart.
I aimed at my own. How perfectly absurd!

In youth I savaged with a flaming love,
in middle age with unforgiving contempt.
The girls all fled, the public dove
under the nearest table at my every attempt.

One year politics like Trotsky drove me,
the next I was the snide aesthete,
then the ridiculous avant-garde loved me
(so I thought), then I rock-starred to defeat.

Experimental novelist, poète maudit,
Beat, then "language," then ranter, free-verse
hipster, then rhymester, neo-anarchist, worse:
postmodern poststructuralist, French, continental,
with a talent uncommercial, not economical—
I was lost to the trends, till the trends lost me.

Today I met one of us, a tweaking poet.

He said, 'You want to save yourself? Lose it.
I was blind, stuffed with rage and spite,
before, at the bottom of the sky, in the dregs,
I saw, at last, the end of the night.

Listen. I'll tell you what I have learned.
There's only one lesson you need to know.
We live to open each other's lives
by baring to each other our own lives. So—

what do we do? We blacken. We burn. We write.' "

The Labyrinth in the Living Room

Vanishing

Have you noticed? Everything is vanishing
into the black hole of information technology forever.
Or so the CPU jockeys like to claim for their singularity,
that hybrid of a cyber-jackass and God,
and I am not being merely sarcastic or tasteless:
it thunders imprecations between earth-shaking brays.

A flag burns methane over the tundra.
The wind lifts the soil from Kansas like a book.
The lunar eclipse is spackled with blood.
A boy bullies a girl with a blackmail hope
and learns the peace of Eros that is despair.
The sun was reduced long ago to a cigarette,
the oceans are boiling down to a scorched tin basin,
and the clouds are smeared flat as an indie bluescreen.

But what of it: they say we will be able to re-create
everything that was anything or nothing at all, my friends,
from silicon, pixels, nuclear processors, and late-night pizza
via CGI and VR, RFIDs and Q-tips
of genetic material swabbed from inside your cheek,
a flake of dry skin from an unlaundered tee—a crumb
of DNA could bring back the whole Precambrian,
a pantry plied with Cretaceous and early Pleistocene
lined up like pies,
with an app to cook up
three billion galaxies in a nanosecond, rub
a proprietary black hole from a nerd's sweaty palm.
Civilizations will be reborn like Japanese paper flowers

blossoming into cities of coral in a cup of green tea
with stars bubbling like bromides in a toothbrush cup
and nature basking in its hologram, the universe.

So don't despair—no, never despair.
Have you noticed?
Everything is vanishing because nothing can disappear.
Maybe only the invisible is eternal.
The rest is crumbling like the wings of Nimrod's lions
in real time on the screen you stare at in your hand.

A YouTube video appears of my best friend in high school.
He died last year. But his video is forever.

They will not stop there. Soon they will invent
a virtual hologram animé
with AI that makes him seem alive—seem alive?
Hell, he'll be alive! Apple
(you have noticed Apple recently became,
for a nanosec,
the world's first trillionaire company!)
well, the world's first trillionaire
must have made its money somehow, and so,
for its next trick to monstrous profit it will introduce,
at some MacWorld of the future,
via (naturally, or rather unnaturally) a virtual Steve Jobs,
the iRobot,
in light and space, chrome and soft synthetics,
that theoretically could be 3D-printed at will—
cloned for as long as the sun burns or until
we bake the world into a gigantic Sahara
with the fossil fuels we forgot to turn into
virtual reality, and the dinosaurs,

in a sense, turn up at last to drink our milkshake,
as we,
our egos, like billionaire teenagers
at their first cocaine party, charging through sound-
 leached space,
demand recognition from the universe,
which yawns and shrugs and slowly turns its back
until even they
vanish.

Self-Identity

Sometimes I self-identify as nothing human,
a broken stick in spring's glass of water,
a trick of the light.

Do not call this a hand;
it's a book of stamps, butterflies, shells
suspended from spider silk above your lap.
When it falls, its wings open
like a falcon's.
Flesh is molten and the screen bleeds
ivory and black.
The hammering you hear
comes from something harder than a heart.
The mirror shows a policeman's
exploding mask.

Look: a glove on a glass table,
the frame for a photograph on an evening desk,
the nib of a ballpoint pen on lined paper,
a library reaching to the end of the night,
a record's repeating hiss on a stereo,
a stare across a parking lot,
a glance at a stationwagon crossing a covered bridge,
a flock of blackbirds floating down the fog,
the sound of laughter across a summer meadow,
a cat brooding,
white storm clouds above a black field,
lightning, soundless, the long wait for the thunder,
a dogwood flowering above my childhood's ashes.

The King of the Web

From flameouts to Facebook and "Comments" to tweets,
joky without laughter and clever without wit,
with pretense to brains torn from panties to nighties,
today's hero can be summed up in one name: "Thersites."

There was once this wonderful thing we had:
it was called (you'll remember) the "world wide web"—
it's, thanks to him, a sewer instead.
(NSA and Thersites and corporate greed:
you will just have to admit, they're quite a bunch:
between them they've eaten the internet's lunch.)

But back to our subject: you will remember
Thersites in Homer, the Iliad, the lowest
soul among the Greeks, a nattering, rabid,
little excuse for a human being,
who invented snark
three millennia before we had a name for it.
A sorry case, he hadn't the discipline
to model himself like clay in fire,
burn the clay in the kiln of mind and will
into something he might, in himself, esteem—
so he had to tear down anybody else
who dared—dared!—appear better than he;
thus he despised them as he despised
himself: *he* was a hateful thing,
so all humanity too must be.

It's a curious being,
smart to a fault, if ill-bred and half-read,

with an enlarged left brain and an unchained mouth:
half monkey, half mule,
a snarky and sorry and squealing and pouty,
sarcastic—what to call it?—
human, in a pinch,
person (with qualifications),
subject,
Dasein,
center of consciousness,
rational entity (with sociopathic tendencies),
id without editor,
unleashed tongue with itchy fingers—
featherless biped and sterile hybrid—
someone who bites the hand that feeds him
and finds two stumps when he finds he needs 'em.
Sometimes a potty, sometimes a dump,
sometimes Thersites, sometimes Trump,
sometimes a cyber-cheerleader called Tay:
he proves it's possible indeed to create
artificial intelligence in analog flesh,
a thoroughly virtual donkey clone.
There's nothing to it but click and bleat
with a squint and a leer, like our gentle cuz
and lord of misrule: a chimp in heat,
a mad dog, a *chien lunatique*
(he's got a lot of cheek!).
He litters the web with pads and spoor,
YouTube has a special place for him
and blogs are snarled with his graceless spats:
his squeals are sometimes mistaken for roars
all the while, as the gentleman grins to himself
as he gnaws on his bone
  "You've got nothing on me!

I see through you all!
I'm nobody's lamb!
I'm not your tool!
I am mine alone!
I am Thersites!
And Thersites, if you please,
is nobody's fool!"

. . . but his own.

Saint Porn

He loved the fantasy, less so the reality.
The smells put him off.
Bodily fluids repelled.
The mechanics he found ridiculous,
the positions absurd.
He felt embarrassed, self-conscious,
half of him felt taken advantage of,
the other half felt like a fool.
On top of everything, he felt guilty,
even when *she* made all the moves—
and for what in the end, he asked himself?
Half the time the girl was lousy in bed;
the other half (as he so painfully knew),
after you sleep with her, she thinks she owns you—
the one to lose respect the next morning is not
her, my poor fellow—it's you.

Sex had a dirty little secret:
it was not unlike everything else in this world—
some of it fine, some just awful,
but most of it mediocre, not bad, not good,
middle-of-the-road, a bore.
Surprise: sex is something of a chore.

How often had he labored to get a girl into bed,
only to discover there mere disillusion?
Sex is an excruciating, long humiliation
from giddy infatuation
to half-mad frustration

by way of an awkward, uncertain tumescence
distracted by a serious fear of deflation;
you feel like the worm in mescal dissolved
as long as a partner is involved.

A light went on when he realized this:
something he'd half-known all along—
having a partner was just wrong.
With dreams protected, fantasies secure
from defeat by reality, its limits, its cheats,
the only reality he let remain
was the one created by his wondrous brain,
brain, that maker of infinite worlds,
a heaven (sometimes hell) between one's ears.
A marvelous discovery: the body's pleasures
were in the control of the human mind:
Sex brought gonads together with brain
in a perfect marriage when one abjured
the fickle partner for a dream
in solitude, enchanted, lorn
never again, and the tranquil grace
of self-sufficiency was born.

He could worship the Body of Woman
in his room's chapel, on the altar of his bed,
in the niche of his computer, its cloistral cell,
send his prayers, make his rites
follow the sacraments of his nights,
study the bibles of eastern thought—
Kama Sutra and Gulistan—
and modern masters Lawrence, Reich,
Harris, Henry Miller, wise
modern Don Juans in disguise,

in guttural and ecstatic tongues
before the sacred mystery
of the body's shining climax,
a mystic indeed of the body,
a religious believer in having sex
with angel lovers, his delights.

Dreams brought love in every sense,
for reality's failure a recompense.
Only now did he feel born,
when he became a monk of porn.

No people resulted, thank heaven for that.
The world, with seven billion and growing,
was driving toward shipwreck in the sea of space.
So his solution to the problem of sex,
in a way, was a public benefit,
hurting no one, content with the reality
of his self-contained sexuality.
To everyone he met he was most kind,
since his body of them nothing desired;
he'd always preferred the life of the mind.
A good life, he thought, contented and quiet:
lightly upon the earth I tread,
and when I die, I'll be really dead;
none of my DNA will stalk the world.
Humanity's modesty begins with me.
Who would have thought true virtue began
with the worship of pornography?

The Young Man Reviews Books on YouTube

"My name is Buford P. Sheetsalot,
And I post (for a fee—I'm a greedy snot!)
    Book reviews on YouTube."
    Even though he's a boob;
    Pontificates on selfies
    Video-captured on unhealthy-
    Looking rooftops in L.A.;
    Like an old-fashioned popinjay,
    Reveres his own musings,
    Neither deep nor amusing;
    Makes pompous avowals
    About a certain "Paul Bowels,"
    Growls like a Pomeranian
    About E. M. Cioran the Romanian;
    Thinks he has wit
    When what comes out … well, *rhymes* with it;
    His "critique" (if that's the word)
    Is to whine "I was bored";
    Thinks he's high class,
    And brays like an ass;
    Calls "Nicer Than Poison"
    His channel: is that so, son?
    Then, please, take some, spare us
    The rest of your errors,
    Pour rather nicer ketchup
    Over the victims of your hatchet:
You'll find it goes so much easier down
Your well-exercised throat as we *cram* it down.

We don't really need
Your maundering screeds,
You'd be better served
If you left to better nerves
And more disciplined intellects
Than your genes did select
To wool-gather in a mind
So ... well ... *un*designed.—
Am I mean? A petty son?
Or just giving him his own medicine?
I merely opine—
And am happily resigned
If the only justice
We can hope for, as for most of us,
Is the poetic kind,
From Mt. Zion or Ararat,
From Parnassus or Camelot,
Whether Neanderthal or Hottentot,
Or wherever we get the rot,
On that pompous, pretentious, presumptuous,
portentous, ridiculous Buford P. Sheetaslot.

Modern Taste

Some think the aftertaste
of modern life
is salty and rank
as dried blood. But
I say not.

The bitter. The dry. The neat.
With one cube of ice.
And a shot of envy.
Suffice, suffice.

Paderewski

Two fistfuls of extravagant hair.
Eyes liquid as mercury, or distant horizons.
A classic profile, delicate and hard.

And those hands—
they bully the ivories
as they might a woman's body,
wrestling the dugs
and sweeping the sweat from her legs.

The keys are like teeth.

The auditorium swooned.

And he stalked offstage in an ecstasy of disgust.

Idiots, he raged.
My hands are red with blood.
They want only body.
To spirit they are nothing,
to music they are dead.

His old teacher said to him, "My boy, not so.
Don't blame them if they take you
for demon or divine.
You bring them messages from another world. Go,
be gentle with them, honor them, bacchantes out of
 their mind.
As dance is goddess in the body

so music is God in the skin.
Your music is from the only divinity they believe in,
it is the only paradise they know."

"If the divinity," the other one snarled, "is part
croupier, part pimp, part drug lord, *I* know!
Don't tell *me*, old lech.
Dance may be purchase of the booty,
but music is the rod in the sin.
I think it's time for me to go."

He hooted and gave his old teach
a grin and valedictory nod,
who furiously blinked, opened his mouth to speak
to a hollow in the air: his pupil had left like a shot.

Victory Cocktail

Heard from a dark hill
in the sweet distance:

dim wild shouts in a rolling roar
like lions the city's pride,

cut by a pounce and crack of cherry bomb
(do they still call them cherry bombs?),
far-away honks and Road Runner beeps
and the throat-clearing of Harley hogs.

Half a dozen voices barrel down the hill,
cheerfully drunk and drunkenly cheering:
"Gi-ants! Gi-ants!"
   (echo fading: "Gi-ants! Gi-ants!")

Dancing in the streets!

The city one huge flash mob
wearing the night like a drunken party hat
cocked merrily askew over one eye

(whisper: Rah! Rah! Rah! Rah!),

the fog clear,
above it the stars, silent, shining.

What Is Literature?

"What," said he, as he sagged heavily
back in his chair by the saloon window, "*was*
literature, is more to the point. Aren't you
glad I'm here to tell you? Alas for both of us—

for I must speak and you, belonging
to the eternal internet generation,
only care to bask in your
hyperlinked 'comments' and exchange of
simpering selfies on Instagram. We were
made for each other, as the saying goes.

Maybe all of it, in the end, was rigged—
yet in all its fantasy, it never lied."

He sighed, raised his glass,
silently toasted the silent room,
took a sip of Wild Turkey, and shrugged.

"In the worlds of matter, energy, chaos,
the permanent slaughterhouse of the marketplace,
the ineluctable, inescapable
Darwinian struggle for what no living
thing in the end can actually achieve—
survival, that mirage in a world of perpetual
transformation—
literature was defiance
of that lame squat, mortality,
soul's defense in the soulless world—

a puff of smoke blown in the face of reality.

Yes, of course, the game was rigged,
but in all its fantasy, it never lied."

He sighed, raised his glass,
silently toasted the silent room,
took a sip of Wild Turkey, and shrugged.

"Writer and reader met on a page
in a corner, away from other eyes,
and built between them fantasies
of a world made for humankind
because made by the human,
enough like the inhuman world
to make them believe it, make them believe
that they might live happily ever after there.

There's no escape if the jig is up.
But in all its fantasy, it never lied."

He sighed, raised his glass,
silently toasted the silent room,
took a sip of Wild Turkey, and shrugged.

"It seized and carried them off
into a verbal sky
in ventures of forever,
snagged on amour and desire,
crushed between wisdom and power;
terrified them with the grandeur
of man when he wrecks his ship,
tickled 'em till they went crazy,

laughed till they choked and wept again,
threw them down till they slept, in twain
shot their hearts across the courts of the moon,
then flashed them past the blackness of the stars.

It gave us paradise and hell,
empires of greed built on love's cold ash
in Paris, London and New York,
the deserts of Bardo and San Francisco,
the place where angels and devils meet,
Las Vegas and Shanghai's shadowless streets.

Whatever could be said it said
in words' infernal heaven,
the cloud-capped victories of language
even if only in a bucket of dust
in a cellar of rusty syllables,

a child's game with its mother's breath,

an old man's dream of what could never be,

an escape for an hour from reality's prison,

a glimpse from our cell
across the loam
of a world that might have been, but wasn't, our home.

And now we have the internet
instead.

The jig is rigged. Oh, if only
in all its fantasy, it never lied!"

He sighed, raised his glass,
silently toasted the silent room,
took a sip of Wild Turkey, and shrugged.

Love Among the Existentialists

The Invention of Fire

One day I heard on a street of this city—
billionnaire ville of high tech and IT,
cultured pearl of Silicon Valley,
capital of the twenty-first century,
San Francisco of the crazed and the crazy—
a man laugh out, "Whatever you do,
or *think* you can, there's one thing you can't do:
you can't disinvent technology!"

But, my darling, what if we could, you and me,
undo the long gold chain of human
marvels and practical disasters, back
to the wild dawn of it all? What if we could
unpave, unpollute, unpoison the world
that we are destroying with our civilized life,
that Frankenstein's monster of silica and code?

—The cell phone suddenly melts in my hand
like a Milky Way bar left too long in the sun.

The laptop wrinkles like an autumn leaf,

the desktop goes up in a puff of smoke
at the sparrow's pass of a magician's wand,
goes up with a smell of burning wood.

Servers curdle like bottles of milk.

GPS goes out like a light.

Monitors line up like dead fish on the sand.

Abruptly vanishes the World Wide Web
like a spider's cobweb catching humans like flies,
and with it the stranglehold of the internet.

A wind picks up over the empty land:
it blows forests of sky dishes away,
flocks of radios, stereophonic herds,
the clotted brainpans of obsessive nerds,
landfills clogged with wireless TVs,
movie cameras, projectors—not those!—yes, those
too—molten flash drives, CPUs,
busses, rockets, snowboards and skis,
rollerblades, Velcro and nonstick pans,
silicon chips reduced to sand,
rare earth metals melting down with smartphones,
the burnt-out husks of intelligent homes,
trains and steamships and telegraphs and sails
crossing the seas like clouds of white whales,
skyscrapers and skylights, iron alloys and glass,
the first lawnmowers smelling of cut grass,
and the central beast at the heart of the wheel:
the million-headed Hydra, the automobile;
the casket elevator, the pick, the spade,
the tackle and hook of a cable of braid,
the IUD, pill, the condom, bidet,
vaginal rings and penis pumps
(the tech of pleasure isn't spared its lumps),
Glocks and anklets, in vitro wombs,
water-sealed coffins and virtual tombs,
robosoldiers, RFIDs, ebola bombs:

the wind of time in reverse sweeping away
everything we invented: the plough, the clock,
the spectacles on the pimpled nose of a monk,
dreadnaughts, all dreading, at long last sunk,
pencil, parchment, typewriter, quill,
propeller, salt cellar, egg-beater, scythe,
horseshoe nail and dentist drill,
uncool self-serve lane and cool Swiss knife:
everything that fell from the war of life
into our far too-clever brains
that are never satisfied and never tire,
back to the beginning of everything until
we lie down again in the mud of a cave
and, snuggling together, as we know best,
disinvent the one we can blame for the rest:
the two sticks that first rubbed together into flame.

See? All gone! It couldn't be done?
We've done it, you and me, in the course
of a little fantasy and, with apologies, verse.
But then, I never needed any of it.
I have needed you, deep as I am in the mire.
Every time we embrace, we invent fire.

Aubade

A cold night in Leningrad, in the depths of Stalin's winter.
A scholar, visiting from England, homely, over-weight, middle-aged,
and an old yet still beautiful Russian poet
talk all night about literature, history,
the Russian writers of the century before,
who nourished them as the Bible did older generations
and would generations to come.
"Pushkin," said the poet.
"Pushkin," said the scholar.
"Chekhov," said the poet.
"Chekhov," said the scholar.
"Turgenev," said the scholar.
The poet gave the scholar a pained look,
then said, "Dostoyevsky."
They were silent, then they both smiled.

The poet talked about her husband,
killed by the Bolsheviks in the '20s,
about her friends—poets, writers, artists—
imprisoned, killed, silenced over the decades
by the leaden avatars of power,
about her son and the daily vigil she kept
for seventeen months
outside the prison where they had taken him,
until at last she gave up.
She recited a poem she had written about that.
Then she offered the scholar tea.
They talked, talked, talked,
walking together across the ice floes of the night.

The sun rose,
and they looked silently outside as the light filtered
through the blinds of her room
like two lovers after a long night of loving.

The scholar left not long after
and walked for hours under an icy sun,
dazzled by the light inside him.
He remembered their fingers had just brushed
once as she served him tea.

The aged poet was harassed, mocked in the press,
publicly rebuked and reviled,
called a slut,
denied access to foreigners
and banished for life from publishing
for consorting, with blatant indecency, with a Western spy.

When the pudgy scholar finally returned to his hotel that morning,
he fell across his bed, half out of breath,
and thought: "I am in love … I am in love."

Botticelli of the Amazon

A painter once lived in Amazonia,
in Bahia, Minas Gerais, Rio, São Paulo—
in the rainforests and on the seacoast of Brazil.
He had painted for many years,
but had grown increasingly discouraged.
He had been seeking the image of goodness,
of wisdom, of grace, of perfect beauty—
but he hadn't found it; indeed found nothing
even close to his inward image of perfection.
And so he vowed to himself
he would not paint again until he found it.

He wandered for many years.
He wandered the jungles, the rivers, the beaches,
the slums and favelas,
wandering across the land he loved—
through teeming cities, old as Cabral
and new as tomorrow's infatuated hopes,
up the furthest estuaries of the Amazon,
to the Andean foothills,
beneath shrieks of parrots and howls of the jaguarundi,
near weed-shrouded pools of piranha,
close to villages of Yanomami
and the gentle homes of Guaraní.

He grew sorrowful—perhaps his ideal
did not exist, had never existed,
or existed only in a different world,
in a different galaxy a billion lightyears away,

a world he would never know.
Maybe he had been a fool to waste his life in the search,
maybe there was nothing to find.

And yet the ideal, smiling kindly at him,
stood, on tiptoe, radiant, in his mind.

His canvases cracked, his paints dried up,
his brushes grew bristly and stiff.
He grew old in his wanderings,
yet still he pushed on.

One day, in his great age,
now near despair,
he took ship to an island
off the coast of Santa Catarina
and went quietly across the island,
and, turning a corner,
or crossing a park,
or walking aimlessly down a beach,
just within sound of the waves,
something caught his eye.
He stopped, and shook his head,
and looked again.

It was you.

His hands, weak and trembling with astonishment,
reached for his almost ruined paints.

Nomad of Love

When first I saw you,
delight sifted down
like snow in a valley,
like sand in a glass,
and the clock turned back
a century,
and for "you" I thought "thou,"
and for "you" I thought "thee."

And the desert burned
past the kitchen door,
and I drifted afar
on the rug of a dream,
and the trail of the sun
vanished—the law
of time was suspended
before this intense
pull toward thee: *hawaa*.

My heart was troubled,
it flamed, it danced
with less joy than fear,
and my dry, parched tongue
could sing nothing, nor speak.
At the core of my chest
was a cough and a laugh,
and a yearning, oh burning
of the heart: *sha'af*.

My mind grew distracted,
it could think hear see
feel nothing else
than your face, voice, breath
against the air, in my mind,
against the weak gate
of my heart,
and I knew I was sick,
trembling, feverish, half dead,
with longing: *'ishq*.

Nor did it stop there:
the trees of the desert
grew tall in the heat,
but they shaded not me:
the sun flew like a hawk
disdaining its prey—
I burned in the sky glass
that filled me with fire,
with ever more deepening, ever more ardent,
intoxicating, demanding
desire: *shawq*.

Oh, how I hoped
as desire rode me
and made my heart soar
between its black wings,
I would find the reward
of tenderness
in the simple confession
before thee: *halaf*.

And at the crown

of that burning day
we would be
oned, together, in passion's
victory,
a drunken dance
of ecstasy,
the thunderhead
in our arms: *gharaam*.

Oh then, I, amazed,
knew I had come
upon the sole treasure
that all men seek,
all women desire,
the jewel, the gold,
the magic lamp's rub,
the breath of the god,
the one perfect good,
the meaning of is,
purpose of will be,
nostalgia's goal:
Love—*hubb*.

Yet more than love;
love more than love
is, if we knew
and admitted it, too:
its victory
is briefly ours
only, it devours,
its law devours,
until there is nothing
left: *law'ah, la'if.*

And then I knew
my fate was signed
like a sentence, life
or death: a slave
to love, convict,
prisoner:
"Want him? Take him!
He's his own no more."
No longer: *taaʻim*.

The joy was short,
the grief was long.
I was sick to the marrow,
I shook in my bed,
my mouth tasted
of tears and blood,
I stank as I sweated:
impotent, able-less,
I was sick with love
unto death: *tabl*.

It was not long after
I lost what was left
of my mind: it went
where my heart had gone—
down a deep hole
and disappeared
in her darkness.
I was sick with despair:
my mind fell like a castle
for I knew that my love
had no hope anywhere.
I went crazy, silly,
babbling: *tadlih*.

And so you now find me,
wandering, distraught,
lost in the streets
of this desert city,
speaking in tongues,
praying to the stars,
mad, wet with tears,
lost, mad: *huyuum*.

I pray in my madness,
as I come, as I go,
pray ardently that we
the love of the god,
divinest love,
thy love for me
as my love for thee,
in future so,
as the clock turns back
to the beginning of time—
the first time I saw thee—
there to find, lo!
our hearts are one,
were always one,
will always one be—
mahubbah.

    If only
to one day know.

Rite of Spring

Your body shines in silence.
Your shoulders are draped with wings.
Your lips are little birds.
Your eyes are star children.

Your breasts are clouds. Your loins
promise heaven in them.
Your hair is a flame, black corona
around your perfect face.

Your perfect face: like a royal coin
cut in bronze, a profile
of chocolate and copper and coffee,
a cameo against the sun.

But in you is a child
gentle, timorous,
who looks out through your eyes
in a kind of startled wonder.

You don't, you cannot, know
your own beauty. "No,
you think, "this can't be me,
this heaven-fallen loveliness."

It holds my mind like the shadow
of a summer shore at twilight
where a monk watches
under a cavern of clouds;

your voice like the sea fog,
muted, soft, vague;
murmurous as the sea,
faithful as a prayer.

Living is hard and filled
with false hope and true bitterness,
but knowing you are here
holds me, holds my heart.

Unseason

In California a lily opens
like a banner. In Brazil
no winter, no autumn: what
rainforest flower welcomed
you into the world? Amazon
forest goddess, your heart a soft
quivering thing like a bird, it sings
a Guaraní song.
Where you walk, the world is spring.

There's Nothing You Can Give Me

I don't already have: imperial
sun, empyrean clouds,
water in the gutter like molten silver.
I don't even need your love
though all the billboards proclaim it.
I have a sleeve of gold on my tongue,
the sky's arm slung over my shoulder.
The forest whispers sweet nothings in my ear.
My love is stronger than both of us
And hurls the earth through blackness.

Bocca Baciata

. . . it hangs forever in the obscurity
of something I barely remember:
midnight hair silken as seawater, eyes glittering,
a tenderness of skin
smooth as the palm of a rose, soft as
cotton blowing in summer, or (I once said, laughing)
as a kitten's belly (at which you growled
like a playful tiger—later the playfulness vanished),
the sweetness of a forgotten world,
all the warm and fragrant hours
we held, once, in our arms:

and the talk! wonderful, about everything
beneath and above and never seen by the sun,
deep, bracing, a harbor of words we shared—
such words!—frank-minded, that ironic heart,
fearless (I learned, not really) soul,
that almost savage spirit:
it was so unbearably beautiful it almost destroyed us.

It did destroy us. A ghost is speaking this.

For we were the unlucky ones,
made from pain and awkwardness, untough,
who could not bear the white-hot coals of love
without breaking and melting into a lump
of proud humiliation;
faint-hearted, easily discouraged; not fearless at all;
disappointed perpetually,

so paying the price in a world made only
for the savage and the brave;
and so we have lived, must live in the half-dark,
sleep in a room made cold to the touch
and hoard our loving in a silent remembrance of love.

And yet it hangs there,
like a single summer's photograph in a wintry life:
a memory, hope's fading inversion,
of those perfect lips,
for once briefly silent, neither speaking nor waiting,
caught in a shock of laughter

that I stopped with our first, and last, kiss.

Café Kabul

At Café Kabul
there is laughter all night,
and the music drowns out
the darkness of the stars.

A couple jumps up
on their chairs and dances,
a table of students
trade jokes like weapons,

an artist makes fun
of his friend the poet,
an old man sings
as the barista grins.

Nobody notices
the regulars much,
who come every day
and stay all night,

sitting in shadow,
staring at their drinks,
making no sound,
listening with strange smiles:

Old Romeo,
who never scored,
Lottery Lena,
who never won,

Tony of the races,
horses running through his dreams,
bitter Maureen,
with her heart in her clutch.

And others too,
sick of TV and web,
come here in the evening
and listen with strange smiles:

there is no love
and there is no hope
and there is no joy
outside Café Kabul.

At Café Kabul,
there is laughter all night,
and the music drowns out
the darkness of the stars.

The Wife of the Painter

She is turning toward you
near the garden window,
in a sunlit dress
and elaborate lace
of the bright eighteenth century,
light and cheerful and demurely
flirtatious
(her hand cupped as if beckoning)
as the enlightenment itself,
near a tumble of flowers
and a wall of darkness—

her face pale and quietly shining,
with its sweetly curved nose
and small lips that barely hide a little
pouty smile, tender and ironic—
as if she has just caught you staring at her
and is about to ask you, "So,
Mr. Ramsay,
am I about to become your next painting?"
And you are about to laugh out loud
and reach for your pencil
and say, "That's it, that's it, my darling! Don't move!"

And you didn't move,
and the painting held you
tenderly
and carried you
down the broken path

between the rose bushes
and the hawthorns,
and the darkening country lanes,
and the gathering seasons,
past the withered garden
and the bitterness of love
and the gravestone in the churchyard corner

to a far country
in the sea-blown light
under other suns
and other skies.

Sleeping Beauty

Locked inside a maniac civilization
hustling between suicide and oblivion,
her face pressed against the glass,
her breathing cannot penetrate the air,
the wind's sheer footprints
stumbling in a perp walk seven billion strong,
the crevasse catching her ankle in its teeth,
the glacier slipping from her bed,
the salt thickening her hair as it rises,
the shadows craning over her cradle
with a railing witch's eyes.

A Beautiful Lie

You say that truth is what you make it,
and that reality is a fraud,
and yet God help those who forsake it
and think truth's bitterness is outlawed:

those fools pay a price. The truth
can have an ugly face and tongue,
though lilacs, kisses, whiskey, sun,
perfumes, flute songs, lovers, strike

scents, shapes, quiverings in the wind,
in stamp and ensign and command,
seducing us who breathe the air
of morning, dream, and reprimand

the blind deniers of the world's grace,
the won't-be-fooled-for-any-price,
the smart, the nobody's-fool, the wise.
There, in high majesty,

star the depths within your eyes,
the moon's arms around your breast,
the bells of laughter of your mind.
Your eyes, like comets in a winter sky,

those lips, two dabs of crayon on a fingertip.
O regal nose!
Seafoam, those cheeks to sleep on, drown in.
A forehead white as a cloud.

Black pride, the winged brows.
Astonishing, that perfect beauty
the spectre Nature gave your face,
yet less than what her majesty
flashes through the mask's astonishment,

through the dancing of your body
like a cloud of rising birds
signaling across the sky
the world's deep, strange tenderness

even as it flies.
Are they so many beautiful lies,
camouflage and sly disguise

that a chromosome puts on
to get itself a replicate
in not-quite-perfect duplicate—

a clone machine in Darwin's hell?
Are you just a vehicle,
when what I see is a miracle?
If so, let truth be damned to hell.

I'll pay—and choose the beautiful lie.

Fado

The moon leaves the night by the backdoor.
The mouse crawls into a mousetrap of hay.
Lupercal takes an egg from his satchel
and breaks it on the bright rim of the day.

"Take that!" cries the rector of Cintra
where he rides the Gadarene swine.
"They will never relent in Aleppo
till we poison the bread and the wine."

"I will never forgive you for leaving me,"
she swore on the book of her loins.
"The arrows of Nepenthe have a sweetness
you will bitterly divine."

A Strindberg of Our Time

"Between the female and myself,
a cold war thrives," he said,
between sucks on his cigarette
and sips of a local wine.
"There is no trust
of love or lust;
we eye the other
like never a lover
in silent derision
of mutual suspicion.

"Yet one or two
I thought I loved,
would have been happy to adore,
if they'd let me.
Which is the crux
of my paradox:
offended, flame-eyed, they showed me the door.

"The reason? Simple:
Though I loved them with a passion
rich, sincere,
kind, generous, good (oh,
don't believe *me*—I'm quoting *them*)
I made it clear
I must refuse
the lock and chain,
the domestic cage
of boyfriend or husband,

obedience to the ovary gate,
their follies,
their petty laws,
respect for their
puerile fears,
the abnegation of my ego,
the pure negation of my brain.

"They sense my contempt
soon enough,
and make no attempt
to win my love;

"*au contraire*:
they flee the rebel.
The air is a wall
of dust from their heels.

"It took me, oh,
ever so long
to *swallow* the truth,
because I am
by nature kind,
generous, open,
unsuspicious,
giving the benefit of every doubt,
patient I am as a stone—
I'm largely a fool
of trust, a softy
to the marrow
of my spine;
and woman is
a cunning fraud;

put her to the proof,
but expect from her anything but the truth.

"I sensed this long ago,
but didn't want to believe it then—
they all of them could not be bad,
so bad, this bad, bad to the core—
with my first girlfriend—a real virago!
With men sex is a sport and a game;
with women sex is a power game,
a drive to conquer and confirm
her dominance in all but name—
let the man run the world
as long as she controls the bed:
Josephine thought Napoleon a fool;
for her no doubt he was.
We will never understand
or control
the little woman

"until we cease to crave them,
and enslave them
with indifference,
the apathy of Caesar
for glittering Cleopatra:
the purity of self-respect,
the hard egotism of the conqueror,
the explorer, the maker,"
he said, with shining eyes, as
he puffed the last of his cigarette
and drank the last of the local wine.
Then he paused,
tossed away the blackened butt
and raised the empty glass to the light.

"But how I do remember
that happy face, those eyes,
that voice I would have given
a world in sacrifice,
my every conquest of the mind,
my so-called brilliance, my glorious genius,
for just a touch of warmth from her,
just one caress—the deep, sweet treachery
of her kiss."

Beauty: A Curse

She was still a striking woman.
We often spoke at length
About life and love, home, friends,
The vicissitudes of family.

One day, while out walking, we passed
A poster for a recent movie:
" 'Mirror, mirror, on the wall,' "
She read aloud as we passed,

" 'Who is the fairest of them all?' "
And she laughed out loud, and looked at me.
"Seeing me now, you won't believe
how once that mirror spoke to me.

I hated it. I hated the face
I saw staring back at me:
A face to take your breath away,
Perfection's beauty.

Not like those *visages* seen
In magazines and Hollywood:
Bland, drab, polished, banal.
No, mine was a wonder:

Exotic and bold and subtle and strange,
It fed you dreams;
It pulled you in, it did not let
You go, it sucked your brains out.

Male, female, it made no difference.
At times even *I* was in love with it:
How could that odalisque be *me*:
Diana, and Athena, and Aphrodite!

It made me laugh.
Then I noticed the world fed back
My look, with wonder and fear and awe
And greed and want and hunger.

Later I learned the price I paid
To give the world the image of
What all men dreamed
And women loathed:

I felt—I felt!—I *was* always,
Always spied on, watched, wanted,
Kissed and lashed by tiny whiplashes
Of longing—I walked down the street

Walled in by eyes,
Desire's glistening nails,
And envy that would kill if it couldn't die.
You don't know what it was like.

I wanted to run away.
Above all I wanted to be unknown,
Unseen, not a desired, and hated,
Eternally hunted prey.

But that was not to be
For many years to come.
And when it did happen …"
She grinned coolly at me.

"But that's the subject
For another conversation . . ."
And we walked on,
Her dry eyes forward.

Love's Labors Lost

He told me one day over coffee.
I had asked him why he seemed so sad.
He looked very surprised. "Not exactly!"
he said, though (I thought) he looked mad.

"You see: I've stopped noticing beautiful women.
Now, is this liberation or loss?
Is it supposed to make a guy like me more human,
or is it just one more nail in my cross?

"For most of my life I loved beauty,
and the beauty of women above all.
Then love broke my heart without pity.
And now, I love nothing at all."

Hotel

A smear of graying hair at my elbow,
she turned to me in the lobby bar:
"You know, I saw heaven once."
"Oh?" I asked. "So, what was it like?"
"What was it like!
It was like rare light on a hand covered with snow.
Yet it charged like a wind of wild horses.

"It swept me across the world,
all its longing charging over the earth
toward ravishments I couldn't measure,
glory and body, singing and dazzling,
joined me in a dovetail to a white star,
ivory and marble and blue as a gift,
all flight, all lift
forever.
Joy? Ecstasy? Stupid words! No words:
it stuffed me with wonder, with silence,
then drove me giddy, down my young loins laughing,
and promised to kill me crazy.
That's what it was like. It wouldn't let me go."
"And then?" She was still. "It let me go.
And down I fell, fell through pits
of cloud, half coal, half ash, flashlights
flickering through slabs of old cars, casually crushed,
ink tags and cartoons smeared with gasoline
like faces of disappeared angels on wet tar,
to a dirty room stinking of Lysol and cigarettes.

"Now I can't remember it. I was there,
I know I was there. But the memory's vague,
and even that's fading fast.
It's strange. Because I can remember hell"—
she smiled at me—"so perfectly."

Divorced Children (a fragment)

They are dreaming.
The sun opens its eye,
and the wind stuffs their mouths,
and the world advances toward them
like an enormous face.
They open the ashes of their arms
as though they are burning wings.
Then they waken . . .

plunging toward the earth.

Midnight

A wash of traffic at the bottom of a neighbor's wall.
Dry rattling of a passing cable car
that carries sleepy travelers to the laps of their hotels
like children who have already forgotten the morning.

Fog a hand's breadth above the towers.
A plane rolling like a broken truck across the sky.

Darkness swarming above the white pyramid like a flock
   of blackbirds.

You keep groping for phrases that might fit
the little column of words in your notebook,
without knowing how or why.
But nothing more comes from the empty sheets
where you lie half-asleep on your bed.

Sweet little nothings, that's all . . .

Grumbling, mysterious night sounds. The cat twitches,
dreaming.
Love never quite happened.
The stillness of the lamplight and the darkness and the
   oceans of the city must be enough.

Poems

win few hearts and change no worlds.
Their words spin out a dream that dissolves
like Splenda on the tongue, dreams that one
must wake from eventually to the irascible day.
They're nice enough a way to kill the time.
Jane Austen said when one was writing a love poem
the passion was just about over. She lied.
Every poem resurrects a love that died.

My love was such a poem, neatly erased,
a night crowded with black stars like eyes,
a death I hoped for, a dream I fought
never to wake from. With my dragon
pen, I burn the sun out of the sky,
and in the night I dream again, again.

The Bright Margin

The disk of the sun
cuts through the horizon
like a knife. Why do I remember you,
your silence, your darkness?

Two birds
flicker across the spires.
Their silence is magnanimous with morning.

Great was that darkness,
greater than anyone knew;
our ember of brightness
rode a bull of iron;
we lived in a tiny room,
overcrowded and angry,
in a great, unlighted city
under a night without star or moon;
our future was soaring
toward a crackup of our own making;
we were locked in Plato's cave
without hope of escape;
our intellectual pride
turned back on us, jeering.

Yet

a single light on a solitary buoy
in the ocean in the night
rocks, rocks, rocks,

and over the shout of the wind
I can hear, faintly,
its bell ringing.

When the sun is in eclipse
its corona flames like hair,
the sun hidden in the light;
its dazzling tiara crowns it
with a bright margin of fire.

The sun breaks time into pieces.

And again you took the gamble,
placed the chips on the wheel of the air.
And across the shadow of the ocean,
you sailed toward the distant fire,

though hope was as much an illusion
in the arms of desire.

Suicide Machine

Modern

He woke in the middle of a nightmare.
The terror lay in his room
like the body of a dead animal
covered with flies. Its teeth
shone in the grass.
                         A French soldier,
half-asleep above the stove of a peasant,
turned, restless with insomnia from his problem:
"What can I know, if anything?"
He knew he could doubt; besides that,
could he know anything at all?

A man raised a tube in Italy
with curious lenses toward the night.
The moon bowed its face toward him.
"What will I see there, if anything?"
To his eye he put the tube and squinted.
"*Cara luna*, will I see anything at all?"

An Englishman sat carefully writing
a work of indisputable logic
through the night. He raised his eyes, reflected:
"What can a man do, if anything?"
In the darkness he heard someone whisper:
"What if he can do anything at all?"

A gentleman in Paris totted up figures
in two columns on a smooth surface of calf-skin:
"What can I make, if anything?"

He counted again: the numbers added up, beautifully.
His fingers grasped the quill so hard it split.
"I can make more. What if I can make it all?"

A thin-lipped, keen-eyed Florentine
stalked the Tuscan hills in the spring,
out of the shadow of ridiculous churches
and the memory of long blood in the streets,
and imagining a Prince to his measure;
murmured to himself,
"What if he could have power over all?"

An ugly Brit bit his tongue
by a late lamp; the darkness was no darker
than his thought: slaughter, war,
human life, vicious, brief, lonely,
and a great autarch to hold in control
the chaos,
"Elsewise it will bring ruin to all."

It was nearing midnight in Europe.
A messenger was crossing the mountains,
taking an urgent notice between sovereigns
who had never met face to face.
As he neared the summit, he stumbled,
his boot dislodging a stone
that fell, gathering more stones as it went
in a wind of rocks, trees, snow,
collapsing across the valley
and a village asleep in its crux
in an avalanche, burying it all.

A Devil's Bargain

The devil came to a man one day
and told him: "I will grant to you
knowledge, wealth and power undreamed of:
every hope mankind has known
will real become, or seem to be
upon the verge of reality
tomorrow or, at very most,
the day after, marvelously.
You will dominate the earth,
take the first steps toward the stars,
walk on the mountains of the moon,
touch the sands on the plains of Mars,
weigh the water on Saturn's moons,
on your fingers wear her rings,
weigh the universe itself
in the scales of your big mind,
measure its length, its breadth, its age,
its time to come, death and old age,
you will be so sage.

"You'll count the smallest elements
that make it up—the quarks, the strings,
the genes, the chromosomes of all things—
and play with them
to make new worlds, new life, new minds—
you'll learn
the origin of space and time,
the source of life, the cause of thought,
everything that can be known
you, and you alone, will know.

"With your opposable thumb, and brain
that Nature in her infinite
munificence gave to marvelous you,
with your gift at math and word,
with your cunning skill of hand,
you will rule the mighty earth—
throw your chains across its seas,
dominate all air and space,
carve the world into a web
of roads that bind great continents,
throw your voice and images
in a mesh of thoughts and cries
until you fill the seas and skies
with nothing but humanity.

"You will need no god but you.
You will be the bright, new god.
You will control reality.
And this will be because of me:
the prince of matter, energy,
reason, cunning, power, will—
le prince de ce monde, in a word;
this world of reason that's perfectly absurd.

"Of course, I ask a little price,
almost nothing compared to what
you'll get in return. You might even say
that what I ask for hardly exists.
I'm almost embarrassed to name it—it
sounds so old fashioned, pre-internet,
so last century, lame, unhip,
for sexless weaklings, ungrown-up,
boring, slow, Neanderthal

as a Republican and as dull
as a Midwestern prayer breakfast:
let's face it: only losers have a soul.
'He'll be talking about God next!'
sneers, in disgust,
those noble virtues of our time,
Selfishness, Arrogance, Gluttony, Greed, and Lust.

"Perhaps. But that is what I ask
in return for a world controlled by you,
a world that will show your ... *interesting* face
where'er you look:
a world of pure reflection,
pure mirror, a marble palace that is
half lunatic asylum, half private prison,
in a lowering tower of trumps.
Yet all of the things you long for most—
life, and youth, and love sans end,
a meaning in the swirl of chaos
of energy and matter—you
will discover are the only things
you're not allowed to have: alone,
mortal, with all your wealth and power,
ingenious devices, every week
tickling you with novelty—
iPod, iPhone, iPad, iLife—
that cut across your existence like a knife,
flattering your infinite vanity,
are nothing but a substitute
for what you cannot have:
something real—
there will be
no meaning, no importance, no

central role in the universe
for you and yours,
however eccentric,
embarrassingly odd, the wish might be
for heaven, hell, eternity,
and that dusty, musty old ghost in the machine called
   God.

"I will make more billionaires
than the world has ever seen before:
a billion bubbles of hot air
that burst till there is nothing there.
And you will see the world you made
is worthless, empty, gaudy, dead:
a corpse dressed in Polo,
Chanel, Versace, svelte brocade
in Italy designed, in Vietnam sewn,
shipped to San Francisco's malls,
to mobs of cool Young Adults sold,
looking forward to a long cruel death, sick, old.

"But I have more: the final end
of my great gift is what your power
will do to the world you've taken over,
wrecking, pillaging, plundering it
under oceans of waste and air
most foul, deserts of famine, unbounded
drought, dead waters rising in
oceanic vomitaria,
with a holocaust of species
that do not serve or entertain you,
then even those you will wipe out,
the net that held you up you'll cut

beneath you, till you've made the globe
a fetid stinking tropic, pole to pole;
the earth you'll have eaten like an apple.

"That is what I offer you:
oblivion and a ransacked world
drifting in space forever
after a few centuries of power and wealth
unimaginably sublime,
based on understanding the facts,
the terrible truth of reality.

"That's my bargain."

The devil fell silent, his hands on the table
next to a paper ready to be signed.
And the man smiled and shook his head
and leaned toward the woman next to him.

"There's no devil and God is dead,"
he whispered to her.
"We are the cleverest things alive.
We'll outwit him whatever he says.
And anyway, it's only a piece of paper.
What do you say?" The woman, concerned,
frowned and asked, "You're sure about this?
It sounds terribly dangerous."
"I'm positive. Whenever did the devil
speak the truth? We already
know most of his secrets.
He's trying to scare us. He wants to keep us
ignorant, weak, under his thumb.
He's full of hot air—most of it

noxious enough! Whatever happens,
we'll be all right." "Hm. Before we
sign our lives away, I have
one little question to ask Mr. Devil."

She turned to Him. "Mr. Devil,
what will happen if we don't sign?"

The devil shrugged. "Nothing at all.
You'll live as you have for 2,000 years
or more: most of you will be illiterate
peasants, a few will serve your lords,
that tiny number
who walk the earth in exalted splendor—
in badly heated palaces, damp
castles warding barbarians off
in pathless forests among impassable mountains
and living in fear of every person,
with nightmares of dagger and poison.
Most of your children will die before six,
your food will be wretched, cost most of your income,
you'll die of diseases before you are forty,
and stink most seasons—especially in summer.
You'll be ruled by idiot kings, bad popes,
and gangster nobles. Crime will kill
those among you who survive the diseases.
Your mind will be
a mire of superstitions, crass
stupidity and prejudice, madness, fear.
You'll be living in the Middle Ages pretty much forever."

"It sounds awful." "But that's how people
lived for thousands of years. It has

one clear advantage." "And what is that?"
"Surviving indefinitely, more or less.
It's what they call a 'sustainable
way of life.' It still killed off
too many other living things
to keep itself fed and amused.
But it might actually last."
                           The woman
thought for a moment and looked at the man,
who looked back, thoroughly appalled.
"Don't listen to him," he whispered hastily
to his virtuous mate. "We can have
everything if we play our cards
right—we just have to be smart about this."
Then remembering the devil's promises,
she held her breath, then said, "All right,
go ahead. Do it. I love you." "It's
a deal," the man said aloud and signed.
His lady added her name too, nicely aligned.

The man grinned, the lady laughed, the devil smiled.
The ink they signed with filled the air
with darkness. "They call me the prince of lies,"
the devil said. "It's not so. I am
the prince of truth. Unhappily for you,
the truth shall not set you free—
it will only reveal more perfectly
the length and strength of the chains that bind you
and the hopelessness of any escape."

The man looked grimly up at him.
"We'll see about that. You have your bargain.
But don't underestimate us, or me.

Humanity
is full of surprises:
just when you think you've got us,
we escape.
Here's my bet: we'll make the world
a garden richer than paradise,
a kingdom of hope and of love, a home
where peace and happiness reign between
man and man, and animal,
and man and woman, his love, his friend.
We shall not conquer the earth, we will
marry it: wed and husband it
with care and tenderness. Love shall win
because it must or we all die:
our final conquest will be man.
Earth shall prevail …"

                                      The devil laughed.
"Hopeless idealist! Blind romantic!
You haven't read much history
or even a newspaper recently.
Good luck with that!" "Good luck indeed,"
the man said coolly. "We all need that."
"You certainly will." "Yes, we will."

They stared at each other across the table.
The ink had not yet dried on the paper.
Suddenly a thought crossed the woman's mind:
"Maybe if I tear it up
right now, it won't be too late…"
But the moment passed.

"Our deal begins?" the devil asked.

"Our deal begins," the man replied.
"We'll see which one's the cleverest,"
the devil smiled as he pocketed the paper.
"It would be a shame to be outwitted
by something that does not even exist!"
And he vanished away in a cloud of smoke and laughter.

The man and woman were now alone.
"What have we done?" the woman said.
"Whatever we've done," the man replied,
"we'll beat him because we must." They kissed.

All You Can Eat at the 21st Century Café

"Hey, beautiful! You quite a dish! Hey gentlemen! Stop
    and talk to me!
Want a good time—hot dancers, radical gambling, a
    foodie paradise, numero uno wine?
Don't let anyone say
you missed the opportunity to have the time
of your entire misspent life, people! Don't regret the
    moment *you* did not seize the *day*!
We got *banquette de* bankster with fresh bonus *mousse*,
CDO *en papillote* served with subprime *profiteroles,*
tar-sand caviar wrapped on a gas frack grill with a side
of chilled SEC inspector *au jus,*
and even a special *menu de finances*
from over-valued stocks *flambés*
to trillion-dollar derivative *surprise.*
We always aim to please!
So come on in! Sit yourself down! And bring a good
    appetite with you!
Greed is good! But gluttony is the best!
So welcome to the 21st Century Café!

"We've got the biggest, baddest feast ever cooked up by
    a mad genius chef—
the Emperors of Cathay
would die for it,
to say nothing of the Caesars of Rome, Mongol Khans,
Japanese Shoguns, Persian Shahs,
Kings of England and Russian Czars!

It's a flatulent banquet with a dish for every taste—
I mean, man it's rad, baby it's the bomb, it's meritorious sir,
    outstanding my man,
c'est magnifique, it's so grand, it's awesome, svelte, neat,
it's so scrumptious it's monomaniacal, it's got scads of mass,
    sass, class and brass—it's the culinary Nobel, it's the Everest
    of feasts,
it's the Orca of eats,
it'll sell, sell, sell, till we all go to hell,
give it to me baby: it will *nev*-vah be beat!
Whatever your background, hankering, desire,
wish, ambition, lust or dream
of any degree, in any facet
of your life, your love, your career or your crimes,
we have got something for You
that will tickle your palate and make you want more:
from *canapés de Narcisse* to billionaire *brulé*,
from stupid celebrity *amuse-bouches* to stake-in-the-heart tartare,
from rumbleguts nectar to chocolate-covered ho'
d'oeuvres, followed by cognac de Koch Brothers and Sarah
    Palin's own recipe for
Baked Alaska!
Everything we've got is so delicious it's meretricious,
it's so bittersweet, uptown savory, expensive tart not cheaply
    acrid,
it will just, I guarantee you, make you want just one bite more;
it's got a finish to last a lifetime and afternotes that will make
    you *come again*, forever!
So don't be shy—come on in—it's the blowout of a lifetime!

"There is only one problem, though,
that maybe you should know
so you can, good folks, decide:

one of our dishes is injected
with a drop of cyanide.
A single bite
will send you to heaven or hell tonight.
And no one has the least idea
which dish it is.

"But not to worry: somebody *else* will eat *that* shit! So:

"Hey, beautiful! You quite a dish! Hey gentlemen! Stop and talk to me!
Want a good time—
hot dancers, radical gambling, a foodie paradise, numero uno wine?
Don't let anyone say
you missed the opportunity to have the time
of your entire misspent life, people! Don't regret the moment
you did not seize the *day*!
So come on in! Sit yourself down! And bring a good appetite with you!
Welcome one and welcome all to the once-in-a-lifetime, end-of-history, final chapter of the human story, so indecent it's obscene, ultimately Anthropocene, suicidal, we're-in-denial, 21st Century Café!"

An Ahumanist

"Who needs atheists?" he said. " '*We*
do not believe in God'? Well, *I*
don't b'lieve in your blessed humanity.
The sooner humans are wiped out,
the sooner the rest of us can rot
in peace."

I was intrigued, if startled. Cool,
he looked, rational, serene.
He smiled wanly. But it was no joke
to him, I could see. Nor did he preen

himself on his intellect or heart,
his courage to face the monstrous worst.
"We are, to put it bluntly,
the condign damnable Nazis of the earth,
her *Kozentrationlagers'* kommandants,
her curse." He looked grimly
around at the rumpled bustling street.

"And so you think we'll have to go?"
I asked tentatively. "Oh yes,
there's no other way." "But who will be
our executioners?" "Alas,

there's the rub: it can only be
us! We'll do it soon enough,
you'll see.
Except we'll take too much of life

along with us on the final ride,
like the last of the great Assyrian kings,
you know, Sardanapalus …

there's a story about him. You know it? " "Not
really, no." "When he died,
he had all of his courtiers killed
and buried with him. He didn't want
to go alone. His tomb was filled

with shrieking concubines, his dogs,
his favorites." He heaved a sigh.
"We're doing something very like. We were
one hell of an evolutionary mistake!
Nature is cursing the monkey for,
in a tryst of thoughtless simian dalliance,
mutating into *Homo sapiens sapiens*!"
He snorted a dry laugh. I stopped listening.
The rain had started. The bus shelter filled
with little shoppers. Their black umbrellas were
glistening.

The faces were worn, worried, blank,
irritated. Just getting through Monday
without disaster—a roof, nice dinner,
a kiss, a hug, a warm bed—was enough for one day.

An old lady hobbled by. A middle-aged man
stared hard into the drizzle. A young mother
dandled a puzzled-looking baby. A teen
made a selfie and posted it immediately on Facebook.

These were the predators of the earth,

these were the conquistadors
of nature, mass murderers, barbarians.
I shook my head. The rain fell steadily.

My brain was tickled by an old jingle
as we all waited for the Geary bus
(he had stopped talking; the rain
ran down his ageing face
like ignored tears)
to take us home before the night
got too cold and wet and dark:

"In their frailty is their power,
in their power is their woe,
if they but knew, if they would know.
Created in a passing hour,
lightly press the world beneath you
like a dance, then lightly go."

The bus grunted to a stop, the doors fell open.

A Mistake Somewhere

We done messed up where we shouldna' messed up.
—Nancy Sinatra

Where? When? Who? What
was the mistake we made, and when did we make it?

Anybody for Descartes? How about Bacon?
Each of those fellows could be said to have launched
the modern world, kicked a pebble that later
loosed the mountain into an avalanche.

Newton, that showoff, shoots up his hand back of the class.
A spitball zings off Kepler's head.
Copernicus looks around nervously;
all eyes are on him.

Then there's Galileo: he looks smug enough,
his telescope tucked casually under his arm:
"E pur si muove!"
Or Leibniz: between him and Isaac, thick as thieves,
the numbers grow like kudzu over a gazebo.

Then Locke wipes the blackboard clean as a rock
and takes the trash out with a smirking, unwashed Hobbes.

They opened a door that maybe should have stayed shut?
Pandora was their mother: trim Voltaire,
Diderot the dancing encyclopedist, d'Holbach, Mettrie,
their obscene master of the revels, the divine Marquis,

Rousseau the lachrymose, who smelled the corpse of God—
he knew there was *something* wrong there—promptly got
hysterical, and gave us his hysteria like a disease.

I. Kant claimed "We can't!"; J. Fichte
hiccupped; Schelling schlept; Hegel
replied, "Maybe *you* can't, Immanuel, but maybe
I con!"
and with that gave a long Bronx cheer:
the Phenomenology of Farts,
the Philosophy of the History of Farts,
the Philosophy of the Right Fart,
to say nothing of the Philosophy of the Aesthetics
of the Fart.

Marx held his nose; however, he saw almost
immediately that
a philosophy of farts, if placed upside down,
would lead to a philosophy of world revolution;
so he drew up a Plan for world revolution
that led about five generations of reasonably
 intelligent people
on several continents, over several cliffs of almost total
 catastrophe
before it occurred to one or two individuals among them
that, hey, maybe there was something wrong
with the Plan. (Oh yes, they call us *Homo sapiens*
because we are so smart!)

Of course, in the United States of America,
as opposed to those decadent, evil, bloodthirsty Europeans,
we had the Founders. They did their best to right
the just-about-to-overturn-and-collapse applecart,

then made us an iron cage that, just when we might like to,
we can't even dream of escaping from.

Adam Smith gave us the invisible hand that holds a noose
choking the necks of generations of scared wage slaves;
then Darwin gave us genocide (*avant la lettre*), and better yet,
gave it a good name! ("It's all part of natural selection,
of Evolution,
of Nature,
so wiping out what doesn't survive—
bats, bees, frogs, dodos, Neanderthals, the human race—
is just peachy.")
Then Schumpeter gave us creative destruction, though he
 forgot to tell
the capitalists about the creative part. "We make profits! Hell!
Who needs anything else?"

The rest was depressingly predictable: Maxwell, Einstein,
Fermi, Oppenheimer, Teller, Kahn,
the Waltons, the Koch Bros., Donald Trump, Steve Jobs,
darling of iDiots
and master of the suicide labor camps of Zhengzhou,
Reagan and Thatcher and dad and son George,
and Rubin and Larry and Timothy and Hank,
the tar sands, fracking, Exxon Mobil, BP,
Blythe Masters, Goldmann-Sachs, the anonymous geek
who wiped away the stock market almost a week
before Greenland's ice melted into the Pond
and turned the seven seas into a lukewarm bouillabaisse
drowning every coastal city from Mumbai to Marseilles.

Mistake after mistake: so, when James Watt saw that steam
could move a machine, then that fellow from Erie, PA,

discovered a foul-smelling black substance just oozing
from the earth that could, along with its bastard cousin, coal,
burn like hell itself, and fuel half the world—
well, it was over.

Ever since, we've been drunk, drugged, blind,
derivative geniuses, idiot-savants of code,
a vast hackers' network of suicidal gods—
Anonymous, Ubiquitous—
hacking, hacking away at the limb we stand on—

clowns on the abyss, a fog of methane plumes
swirling around us as the last glaciers collapse,

and us dancing like it's 1999 forever . . .

(Bollywood conclusion to life on earth, all of humanity
   dancing to really bad, but catchy, music,
as

a bone whistles annihilation to a howling dog.)

Blithe Master

clever conjoiner of our ambitions
creator of nothing out of everything, queen of bulls
daughter of kong

inventor of the derivative
immaterial dictator with the face of Quixote
magnificent acrobat of the perilous mountains

plagiarist of reality
destroyer, like Shiva, of worlds

cantankerous inheritor of the towers of Dubai
despiser of the querulous PC

empress of life, of death,
depending on your reassignment of the hour

master of the revels of the night

menace at 4 a.m., leftward tilt
of the meat clock defamation
and reprisal

inchoate toad insignia of failure
skinless deadbeat

crux of Darwin, Freud, Ricardo, Thorstein Veblen and
Peter Pan

griot in the wine-dark sea off the Congo coast

o forever blithe master

doom lord of the north star stock, bond, CDO portfolio
master of the nanosecond suicide IPO
builder of Paradise where the forests will burn
in conflagrations that shall melt the sky
to the bones of Nineveh, Shanghai, London, New York
and the white talons of Ur
(o master)

regicide, perpetual pretender,
prosecuting attorney
in the courts of sin, Polo shirts and enhanced
interrogation techniques
laughing master

criminal alibi, molten fingers of bliss
on the throat of a homeless woman
prancing naked on the Twitter sidewalk
dancing master

camera oscura of despair
in the darkness of the silicon chip
where all things shall be crushed
unto the next singularity
o naked, singing master

fear no more our sinister giddiness, just
shimmy on the hot embers
till your feet char
and the smell of skin burning charms your senses,

my ever cunning master

then fly, fly, fly above Luna Park
screaming your scream of victory
like a petrel
my master, my own master

crammed with a sun as hot as night,
animals madder than women or men,
and drown in floods of seawater
as the oceans stink like a grave

then destroy it all in a blind flash crash

blithe master,
you happy one,
as you ride the world,
like the Thunderbolt,
shrieking

How to Deal with the Brothers Koke

The why is patent now,
the only question how.

With a knife, with a Glock, with a choke?
What should we do about Caca y Loco Coke?

(Caca y Loco, Loco y Caca:
it hardly makes a difference in this fracas.)

With money?
Oh, that's funny.

With votes?
Don't be a dope.

Poison?
Will get you in prison.

With a gun?
Depends on the Supreme Court. Though, hell, it might be fun.

Maybe draw and quarter,
then feed'em, a piece at a time, to a piranha-filled river,

force feed'em with vodka till their iddy-biddy livers
give up the ghost with a mighty temblor of quivers?

Flay them with sleek horsewhips of laughter
till they beg and plead for their own slaughter?

Hang'em? Impale'em? Skin'em alive?
Fry'em? No, too Quentin Tarantino. No, I've

a better solution: stick
Loco Coke alone in the softening Arctic

whiteness under six months of sun
where there is nowhere on earth to run

as the ice crumbles like stale cake under his feet
till he squeals in a sun-crazed howl of defeat,

sunk in rotting tundra, plumes of methane,
a stench, suffocating even a Koke's genius brain,

as Inuit folk who have lost whole towns, lost a home
to the dying ice, circle in their kayaks and curse him,

and he's surrounded by famished polar bears,
staring at him like he was a chocolate éclair

and they were shopping matrons in a pastry shop
after a long day shopping, and they lick their chops

till he screams: "All right! You win! Stop! The planet
is heating up! Just get me out of this, dammit!"

And where will Bro Caca be in all of this mess?
Brother Caca thinks he couldn't give a whit less.

"Loco was always loco." He's hanging out in Wichita
thinking he will have the last haha

as Kansas crisps into a vast cornflake
toasted black, poor state, as it silently bakes;

he always was absurd, come on, let's admit it,
there's not much difference between him and a … nit-wit.

(What did you think I was going to say?)

Loco y Caca: there's nowhere to go, hermanos.
That is your—and our—woe. Vamos!

Salt

Five billion.

Years, if one can call them that,
before there was any to measure them.
The number itself a hopeless fling
toward the futile husks of knowledge.

No, I can't grasp it.
One is dignified, calm.
Two is charged with life,
a dozen is almost cozy,
a hundred has heft,
a thousand has grandeur;
a million inspires awe.
But a billion . . . !
Nothing!
The mind curls up in a ball and goes blank.

Raining light on the earth,
like a third degree,
vastnesses of light
out of greater vastnesses of darkness.
Until a crystal forest,
with immeasurable slowness,
thrust its head from the ground
and raised its face—its many faces—
above a perpetually drunken earth
spinning like a Sufi in the darkness.

Between a vice of rock and light,
between the hammers of past and future,
darkness presses into diamonds
microbes, birds, civilizations,
a quantum of memes, fugue of poems,
triumphs, extinctions. The dancing
and singing of the sun,
itself even older
by billions
upon
billions
of
years
(the brain aches),
in a universe even older than that,
and what of the multiverse!—

like a scratch of falling star across the eyelid of the night,

like crumbs of salt dropped into a pot,
with enough time, just, for each to say,
turning to each other before dissolving, "I loved you."

No, I cannot grasp it.
Perhaps I wasn't meant to.
Perhaps I was only meant to sleep,
like my cat most of the day,
like you who sleep through the long night of your life,
twitching and stirring under the flight of dreams,
the salt dissolving sweetly on your tongue.

War Poem

He takes the clock in his fist.
Sirens cover the laughter
on the other side of the river.
The air limps over the field.
Squadrons loom through the marsh fog
and search beams strip the sky
of long remnants of light.
His other hand cuts out the springs,
and time scatters, like pennies
from a child's piggy bank,
the coins dark as scabs.
The grunts rush across the meadows.
If only it were a question of burying
the numb memory of the fever,
but not quite. On the contrary.
It is the command of the monarch,
the chrysalis in the congress of iron,
failed drugs, mutant diseases,
minds picking souls from the gardens like daffodils,
and the curling slab of a history book
burning in a bowl on the ice
in the winter twilight.
History is peculiar. It seems unbearable,
and is all we are certain to leave behind.
Here are the words you left.
They burn under history like a pair of hands.

The Hound of Afghanistan

It rages in Helmand
it gnaws a bone in Kandahar
it buries its fangs in the neck of Kabul
in Tora Bora in Herat in Mazar-e Sharif
in the poppy fields of the Pashtun
it is made of dust and mountains and horses
    and the madness of young men and stars
it stands howling in the Khyber Pass
its mouth is red with the blood of 10,000 years
   of invaders
the invaders that are dust that were dust that
   will be dust beneath its paws that dig
when killed it rises again in its hundreds
the bones of Alexander walk crying in the night
the Taliban are a mere fang in its jaws
they too will perish
like the monuments of Buddha and dust that
   they made perish
the Greeks the Romans the Persians the Moghuls
   the British the Russians the Americans al-Qaeda
   the Taliban
stumble blind and mad toward the mad dog
   of Afghanistan
that will not be conquered
though the women and children weep with
   praying hands

Eyeless in Gaza

Strong, blind, he stumbles over the broken land.
His teeth are black. Boots crush a few innocents.
What does he care? His old wounds crowd his mind.
"Make everyone pay! Who pitied me? No pity!
Kill the children! Kill the mothers! Kill the men,
above all, who blinded me! Wipe them out!"
His fists hurl through the darkness.
                                            The YouTube
videos
show children
left behind his boot,
sand packed in their eyes, crusting their lips like dirty
glitter,
the black-scarved mothers hysterical with grief,
the sunlight like a scar.

No pity, no pity—an eye for an eye,
and the whole world has gone blind. Evil
stalks men. It eats them. Then it spits them out.

Pity
       everyone,
              all of us—

or who shall pity us?

Six Animal Songs from the Gone World

1. Mastodon

Long gone
the mastodon,
a bone
in a museum,
a tusk
the size of a rocket
trying to dance the merengue,
a head
the size of an elephant.

Big brother to the elephant,
once great in the Pleistocene ice age,
now a slip of powder in a dried-up riverbed,
a silhouette in a tar pit, petrified, and not from terror
    only,
a rendering on a natural history website.
He lifts his great trunk,
mighty hose of august power,
and trumpets over the plains.
BLARE!
Who are those two-legged pipsqueaks
coming to needle me with their pins?
Who do they think they are?
My conqueror?
Hah!
BLARE!

He was dug up ten millennia later,
a spearhead buried in his eye.

2. Giant Sloth

Well?
Who needs to move?
I say my way
is the way of plenty.
I sleep all day,
when I dream I play:
*si dolce far
niente.*

The world's a mess
of *more* that is in fact
less.
You move too much,
Tovarich.
Settle down,
you spastic clown,
there's too much jazz,
you American spazz.
Think you'll beat the sun?
Can you never forget?
Who are you trying to save?
The faster you run
the sooner you get
to your grave.

I learned the secret
of happiness:

hang over the world
like a cloud over a stream,
move little
and look like a stump,
and let life turn into a dream.

We grew so big
millennia ago
that even lions kept their distance.
Then humans came;
we were never the same.
Ants with brains,
mosquitoes with guns,
a mouse with his little mouse hand on a nuclear bomb,
a spider strangling in his own web hanging from a dusty
   beam.
Nothing could keep
them down.
You've got to admire them,
the clever fools,
They wiped us out.
They think they survived.

But no one survives.
The game called Life
ends in a draw.
Nobody wins;
the losers are the ones who think they can.
You may as well dream
until you fall, like a very heavy leaf, into the stream.

Yes, I know: that sort of
fatalism

is hopelessly un-American.
But sloths are un-American by nature!
Even Giant Sloths, bigger than the biggest SUV!

Now, if you don't mind, I think I'll go back to sleep.

3. Great Auk

I am the ghost of the last auk.
The moment I died was the moment I was not born.
A paradox? Listen.

Three hunters—
Jon Brandsson, Ketil Ketilsson and Sigurdur Iselfsson—
came from Reykjavik to the isle of Eldey,
where my parents lived, in the cold Atlantic
under the harsh sun
and the spangled wind
among thriving banks of cod
and glittering flocks of gulls.

My parents were the last auk couple,
and I lay curled up in their last egg.
It was, by the human calendar, June 1844,
for us it was a season of high sun and no snow
between the seasons of thunder and darkness.

I had lain in my egg for almost a year
and heard the passing storms through my shell
and saw the light from each day come and vanish,
and felt the warmth of my mother's feathery down,
and heard my parents chortle and squawk,

but all very dimly.
Jon Brandsson, Ketil Ketilsson and Sigurdur Iselfsson
came in a rowboat to our island
in search of auk to sell to a dealer
who promised them nine pounds sterling
for two dead birds.
The men landed on Eldey,
and my parents, knowing the wanton murderousness of humans,
fled across the rocks.
But they were too slow.
The men gave chase,
and in a few minutes
caught
and strangled them.

While running after them,
one of the men
(I think it was Sigurdur Iselfsson)
stumbled over what he thought
was an oddly shaped rock on the beach.
My egg was only a few days from breaking,
and I had already begun testing the shell
with my little beak,
chipping away at the inside wall,
when suddenly it burst open
like a long-locked cage,
and I had a blinding glimpse of the startling sun,
and heard the sweet roar of the crashing sea,
and felt a caress of wind across my down,
and heard the sound of my parents squawking in terror,
and saw the sole of the boot of a man
before, as I was not born, I died.

The men rowed away with the bodies of my parents.

The gulls scream above the island,
and the waves crash on nights of storm,
and my spirit is left alone on the isle of Eldey,
and the fragments of my shell are ground into grains of sand.

I pity them, Jon Brandsson and Ketil Ketilsson and Sigurdur Iselfsson.
Annihilation is terrible,
but it is even more terrible
to be its cause.

4. Luci, the Little Brown Bat

She could almost fit into your palm.
She hangs like a leaf
embrowned by autumn
from a cranny in the cave of Aeolus.

In ranks they hang
like fruit in a greenhouse,
but a greenhouse that is cold with winter.
On their noses are spots of white
like snow.
When they stretch their wings in their sleep
their wings are dotted with more motley of white:
it looks like powdered sugar on ladies' fingers.
They are sleeping.

Who could have known
the fungus would come
from someone's respectful visit to the cave?
Like a bedbug carried in a backpack,
or a seed in the lining of a laptop sleeve,
or a slurry of jellyfish, corals, kelp, sandsharks
in the belly of a tanker crossing the Caribbean Sea.

The great reshuffling has commenced.
Not even the luci,
as she rushes, among a storm of wings, out of her cave,
her little squeaks shrieking across the black air,
can see her way to the end of that darkness.

5. The Bearded Saki

Eyes the color of jade.
A look on its face, alert, half-worried,
the long waggle of fur on its chin
solemn as a sage's.
Its tail is fluffed up like a frightened cat's.
"Who are you?" it seems to ask.
"Should I run? But where could I run to?
Is there anywhere I can hide from you?
Or maybe you will not destroy me
after all?"

Something catapults into the trees behind it,
the sound of its chattering disappearing up the jungle
   mountain—
its mate perhaps;
as if thinking escape is possible

and believing in the wisdom of flight and of fear.
But the saki stays there staring solemnly at me
as if waiting to hear my reply.

6. A Golden Frog

"My princess—you kissed me
on the nose, like a pampered dog,
and I turned, not into a prince but a puddle
of yellow speckled with black."

The princess laughed.

"My small shining body
winked in the shadows of the wilderness,
winked and gave to everyone
and to all good luck."

The princess smiled.

"Then
I ceased. From the wilderness
I have vanished, my princess.
What charm did I have then
and now lack?"

The princess frowned.

"Have you no regret?
Why did you forget?
Is this forever? Or not yet?

I have vanished in the fog.
I am gone, golden frog.
I am now only a prince of ghosts."

The princess wept.

Ripped from the Annals

                    enacts the hysteria of the modern,
a culture that lets nothing settle,
unless you impose your will—can you
impose your will? the modern dissolves every statement
into a question, questions are a disease,
are questions a disease? in the hurricane of disavowals
there is only one absolute,
there can be no end to disavowals,
hysterica passio is our abiding

lace hangs from the rafters among over-ripe papayas and
   stale cigars
found by tourists wintering in the Caribbean
and filling the smoke-filled internet with dreams,
a terrified child fends them off with his shoe
and a bow tipped with pale arrowheads
lost in the Black Hills—his dreams will be his own.

So what, you say? It's an illiberal press
that lies in the cradle and profits from the grave.

But you knew all this already,
a southern spy in our jungle wrought
from the jeremiads of the nation,
the bromides of the times

broken wings, crippled angels of Venosa and Assisi,
a sacristy opens to the songs of nightingales,
their wings darken the ruined vestry,

an underpass floods with spring snow,
variants of disease, emollients of the future,
an inkwell bursts with clouds of locusts,
a scholarly Jezebel crouched on the horizon,
screaming down signs with scornful exegeses,
and a pale blue lattice shows a rose
blossoming into flames in the shattered greenhouse,
where I met you once, that late autumn evening,
and we confided nothing to each other,
there was no trust between men and women in that country.

On it goes, crumbling in random flourishes
like fireworks glowing in your hands,
the flash from the explosion taking almost forever to arrive

you impose your will
questions are a disease
(can there be no end to disavowals?)
the rose breaks through the greenhouse toward the sky

When the young, brash Alexander the Great, after putting all of Greece under his tutelage, visited Athens, the one Athenian he wanted to meet was the philosopher Diogenes—also known as Diogenes the Cynic, or Dog, because, out of contempt for civilization and its luxury, dishonesty and self-adoration, he lived a life of such simplicity many people thought it was no better than a dog's. Others considered him the wisest man in Greece.

Alexander found Diogenes sitting at the side of Athens' agora, and going up to him and standing between the celebrated ascetic and the sun, the future conqueror of half the world asked if there was anything he might do for him.

Diogenes, who was sitting half naked on the ground, with his only possessions—a tub and his loincloth—thought for a moment, then looked up at Alexander and said:

"Yes. You can get out of my light."

For Keiko

ABOUT THE AUTHOR

Christopher Bernard writes fiction, poetry, essays, plays and criticism. He is co-editor of *Caveat Lector* and a regular contributor to *Synchronized Chaos*. His poetry can be found online at The Bog of St. Philinte. He lives in San Francisco.

www.ingramcontent.com/pod-product-compliance
Lightning Source LLC
Chambersburg PA
CBHW030528080526
44586CB00011B/355